MURPHY'S LAWS of PARENTING

BY STEVE DENNIE and ROB SUGGS

INTERVARSITY PRESS
DOWNERS GROVE, ILLINOIS 60515

InterVarsity Press® is the book-publishing division of InterVarsity Christian Fellowship®, a student movement active on campus at hundreds of universities, colleges and schools of nursing in the United States of America, and a member movement of the International Fellowship of Evangelical Students. For information about local and regional activities, write Public Relations Dept., InterVarsity Christian Fellowship, 6400 Schroeder Rd., P.O. Box 7895, Madison, WI 53707-7895.

Cover illustration: Rob Suggs

ISBN 0-8308-1839-1

Printed in the United States of America ∞

Library of Congress Cataloging-in-Publication Data
Dennie, Steve, 1956-
    Murphy's laws of parenting/Steve Dennie and Rob Suggs.
        p.   cm.
    ISBN 0-8308-1839-1
    1. Parenting—Humor.   2. Child rearing—Humor.   I. Suggs, Rob.
II. Title.
PN6231.P2D46   1993
818'.5402—dc20   93-41358
                                              CIP

17	16	15	14	13	12	11	10	9	8	7	6	5	4	3	2	1
08	07	06	05	04	03	02	01	00	99	98	97	96	95	94		

Contents

Introduction
1. The Conceptual Murphy
2. Murphy Rocks the Cradle
3. Murphy in Preschool
4. Murphy R Us
5. The Messy Murphy
6. Murphy Goes to the Principal
7. Murphy Gets in a Fight
8. Murphy the Menace
9. The Exasperated Murphy
10. Murphy on Vacation
11. Murphy Knows Best
12. Murphy Becomes a Teen
13. Murphy 90210

Introduction

Murphy's Law states, "If anything can go wrong, it will." This certainly applies to the fine art of parenting, which always follows the path of least logic and order.

Murphy's Law lurks nearby when:

☐ everyone is waiting impatiently to open Christmas presents while Dad searches the house for the camera flash attachment.

☐ the car breaks down on the way to a school program.

☐ your talented preschooler draws a beautiful crayon picture . . . on your wall.

☐ Junior fills the keyhole with Play-Doh.

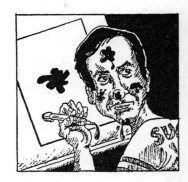

The branch of philosophy known as Murphology includes hundreds of laws, axioms, theories, corollaries, rules and syndromes which show Murphy at work in all realms of life. But not enough attention has been devoted to the family, where Murphy afflicts more people more often than in any other setting.

Until now, that is.

Steve Dennie & Rob Suggs

1 / The Conceptual Murphy

The Nine-Month Law

It doesn't get any easier.

The Mother's Comfort Corollary:
Not even pregnancy lasts forever.

Extension:
While pregnancy doesn't last forever,
motherhood does.

Fullness of Time Determinants

Pregnancy occurs after:

- ☐ You reach your dieting goal.
- ☐ You buy an expensive new outfit.
- ☐ You begin telling people that you don't plan to have any more children.
- ☐ You land your dream job.
- ☐ You turn your extra bedroom into a den.
- ☐ You start using birth control.
- ☐ You adopt.

Law of the Goodwill Box

Throwing away the old baby clothes increases the chance of conception.

Corollary:
If you keep baby girls' clothes, you'll have a boy. If you keep baby boys' clothes, you'll have a girl.

Corollary:
If you keep baby boys' and girls' clothes, a friend will have twins of different sexes, and you'll give her all of your baby clothes—and then you will get pregnant.

The Deer/Dearest Conflict

The due date will be on the first day of hunting season.

Admonition:
This is not something a husband can blame on the wife.

The Down-sizing Dilemma

By the time you can fit into your new swimsuit, it will be out of style.

Corollary:
Or you'll get pregnant again.

Futility Addendum:
The thing's never going to fit, so just get rid of it.

The Quiver Postulate

You never have the number of kids you want.

Murphy's Law of Geometric Infantilism

The predominance of Murphy's Law doubles with the addition of each child.

The Law of Errant Spousal Perception

The husband's "easy delivery" is the wife's "I thought I'd *die!*"

⇦ Principles of Christening

Parents with unusual names (like Tabitha and Joshua) give their kids common names (like David and Sue).

Parents with common names give their kids unusual names.

Addition:
No matter what the name, a child won't like it.

Mike's Theory of Gender Redundancy: If you have three daughters and decide to have one more child, it will be a daughter.

2 / Murphy Rocks the Cradle

Motherhood's Bane

Taking care of a baby is easy if:

☐ you don't require any sleep.

☐ the baby belongs to someone else.

☐ you are the father.

First Law of Sleep ⇨ Deprivation

Your sleeping child will wake up when you decide to lie down for a nap.

Second Law of Sleep Deprivation

The chance of the baby crying in the night increases with the busyness of the next day.

Hoobler's Corollary:

There is a direct correlation between the amount of sleep you need and the amount of late-night and early-morning play time your baby needs.

Third Law of Sleep Deprivation

When the baby finally falls asleep, the phone will ring.

Fourth Law of Sleep Deprivation

Your baby will go to sleep one hour before you have to get up.

Fifth Law of Sleep Deprivation

When you finally fall asleep, the baby will wake up and want to be fed.

Rules for Pew-Bound Infants

Taking a baby into the sanctuary causes it to cry.

Taking a baby out of the sanctuary causes it to cry harder.

If your baby quiets down and you return to the sanctuary, crying will resume.

At the quietest point in the service, your child will burp.

When the Spirit moves, someone's kid squeals.

The rowdier the kids, the greater the chance the parents will sit in the front of the sanctuary.

Ask not for which parent the frustrated nursery worker cometh during the middle of the service. She cometh for you.

The Oops Factor ⇨

Babies only vomit in the direction of clean clothes.

Theory of the Unanticipated Accident

No matter how long the trip, you will pack one less diaper than you will need.

The Proximity Proverb

Whining is in the ears of the holder.

The Gender Misdiagnosis

Dressing your baby daughter in a pink dress with a frilly bonnet won't stop people from exclaiming, "He's so cute!"

3 / **Murphy in Preschool**

The Bigmouth Admission

If one child is singing loud and off-key in the Christmas program, it will be yours.

The Frostbite Formula

The colder the weather, the greater the chance your child will bite holes in his mittens.

The 505 Dalmatians Scenario

If you babysit five children, and each brings a videocassette of *101 Dalmatians,* you will have to watch all five copies.

Potty Postulates

Potty-time occurs as a direct result of:

☐ Bundling your kid in a snowsuit, coat, scarf, mittens, face mask, and boots.

☐ Getting in the car for a trip.

☐ Going to bed.

☐ Posing for a photographer.

☐ Reaching the front of the Great America roller coaster ride after waiting in line for an hour on a scorching hot day.

☐ Driving one mile past a rest stop, with the next rest stop 60 miles away.

☐ Changing the bed sheets.

☐ The whole family is at the theater, and you're at the best part of the movie, and it just can't wait.

The Dustball ⇨ Tendency

The dirtier the object, the greater the chance it will enter your child's mouth.

The Toddler Translation

"Wait!" means "Go!"

Mikey's Maxim ⇨

Children will try anything if you put frosting on it.

Corollary:
Or tell them, "This isn't good for you."

The Gotta Go Far Rule

When you reach the section of the mall farthest from a public restroom, your child will need to go.

Extension:
By the time you return to the previous location to resume shopping, nature will call again.

4 / Murphy R Us

The Law of Childhood Revisited

Parents buy their children the toys they always wanted as a child but never got.

Corollary:
Toys you liked as a kid are never the ones your own kids will like.

The Overflowing Toybox Conclusion

The more toys a child has, the more the child wants.

Corollary:
Kid have. Kid want more.

Corollary:
The more toys a child has, the less enjoyment each toy gives.

The Lapsed Attention Proposition

Children lose interest in items when it's too late to return them to the store.

Mom's Excavation Kit

If you're missing a piece of your heirloom silverware, it will inevitably be found in the sandbox.

Principle of Sharing: In any playroom, a child will want a toy already in the hands of another child.

The Mr. Magnavox Rule

Before going outside to play, children will turn on the TV.

Corollary:
If the TV is already on, they will turn up the volume.

The Deluxe Swingset Theory

The more expensive the toy, the less children like it.

Corollary:
The more expensive the toy, the greater the chance it will be used once and then discarded.

The Squirt Gun Principle

The more breakable the toy, the more the kid will want it.

First Rule of Gift-Bearing Relatives ⇨

Visiting relatives will bring your child the loudest toy they can find, and then leave.

Second Rule of Gift-Bearing Relatives

Visiting relatives will bring your child toys which take four batteries—and you have none.

The Annoyance Factor

Loud toys endure forever.

Corollary:
Quiet toys require batteries, which quickly run down.

The Weather Inversion Principle

If it's sunny, they'll want to play inside.
If it's rainy, they'll want to play outside.

The Law of Jacks

The sharper the lost toy, the greater the chance it will be found by your bare feet.

The Lucky Charms ⇨ Observation

Toys buried in the bottom of cereal boxes mysteriously rise to the top when the box is opened.

The Ronco Comparison

The amount of TV advertising given to a toy is inversely proportional to its quality.

5 / The Messy Murphy

The Amplified Chaos Axiom

No room is so messy that it can't be made worse by telling your child to clean it up.

Cheryl's Addition:
Children clean their rooms by stuffing everything under the bed or in the closet.

First Rule of Spills

Wiping the floor causes children to spill milk.

Second Rule of Spills

The Scotchgard on your furniture won't work with whatever your children spill.

Third Rule of Spills

Stainless food never spills.

Fourth Rule of Spills

White Easter outfits magnetically attract red Kool-Aid.

The Like Mother/Not ⇨ Like Daughter Rule

Meticulous moms raise messy children.

Hoobler's Laws of Family Keepsakes

Putting family keepsakes in the attic causes the roof to leak.

Putting family keepsakes in the basement causes the basement to flood.

The best protection for a box of family keepsakes is to write "junk" on it.

The Safety Fallacy

Childproof containers aren't.

Corollary:
Childproof containers are parent-proof.

The Soap Aversion Postulate

Holding a washcloth makes children physically incapable of reaching behind their ears.

Law of Earth Displacement

Children and the mud on their shoes are soon parted . . . on your clean carpet.

The Dropsie Principle

Fate, when deciding which dish your child will break, always chooses an expensive one.

The Law of Pepperoni ⇨ Decay

The last piece of yesterday's pizza is on a paper plate underneath the couch and won't be found for two weeks.

Law of the Lens

The newer the eyeglasses, the more susceptible they are to scratches.

The Narrow Aisle ⇨ Maxim

Children in shopping carts can always reach shelves filled with breakable bottles, usually containing mayonnaise.

The Smudge Theory

White hallway walls attract the dirty hands of children passing through.

The Crayola Principle

Red and yellow, black and white, your child will want to take a bite.

The Housecleaning Statute

Although Rome was not built in a day, the neighbor kids could trash it in an hour.

The Clutter Tendency

Children's tricycles and other toys always end up in the middle of the garage floor, to be discovered—and moved—by you upon returning from work.

6 / Murphy Goes to the Principal

The Hectic Parent Truism

The farther you live from the school, the more involved your child will be in extracurricular activities.

Corollary:
Extracurricular activities are timed so as to cause you the most inconvenience and drive-time.

The Super Mom Conflict

Your third-grader and seventh-grader will be involved in musicals at two different schools on the same night.

The Law of Aspired Pride: Only other people's kids get straight A's.   Corollary: They live next door.

The Homework Equation

Amount of homework assigned: n.

Amount of homework actually taken home: $n - 10$ minutes.

Amount of homework admitted to parents: $n - 20$ minutes.

Amount of homework actually completed: $n - 30$ minutes.

Law of Forgotten Homework

The longer you spend helping your children with their homework, the greater the chance it will be left on the kitchen table the next morning.

Corollary:
By the time you drive to school with the homework, the teacher will already have collected the assignments.

The Cowabunga Principle

A child who can't memorize the times tables can memorize the script of *Teenage Mutant Ninja Turtles*.

The Impromptu Chaperon Principle

The night before a school field trip, your child will remember that you were supposed to go along as chaperon.

The Sign of the Tell-Tale Scrawl ⇨

That's not necessarily your signature on the excuse note turned in to the teacher.

The Dutiful Father's Frustration

Your child's two-line part in a school play will fall on the day of the seventh game of the World Series.

Dear Teacher: Please Xcuse my SuN =BINKY= FRom The SPeLinG Bea Cuz he has a BRaiN N-juRy. My Mom

The Simple Math ⇨ Paradox

Today's arithmetic methods are incomprehensible to today's parents.

The Fog Alert Rule

School and bus delays occur on days when you need to get to work early.

Law of Parental Notification

The more important the school note, the less likely it will reach home.

The Growth Spurt Phenomenon

The more expensive the outfit, the sooner your child will outgrow it.

Law of Shredded Bugle Boys

Your child's desire for a clothing item increases with the number of holes.

Corollary:
The cost of children's clothing increases with the number of holes.

The Theory of Reversed Aspirations

A child who wants to become a garbage collector will grow up to be a doctor.
A child who wants to become a doctor will grow up to be a garbage collector.

7 / Murphy Gets in a Fight

The Law of the Other Parents

Billy's mom doesn't really allow it—but it sure sounds good.

The Law of the Leftover Oreo

The number of cookies is never divisible by the number of children.

The First Eternal ⇨ Certitude

Mother knows best.

Corollary:
Children don't believe this until they become parents.

Equal Time Addition:
Father knows sports.

The Second Eternal Certitude

Mom always finds out.

Corollary:
Dad always finds the remote.

The Big Brother ⇨ Contention

It's always the little brother's fault.

Corollary:
Is not.

Corollary:
Is too.

The Law of Spontaneous Combustion

Siblings don't need a reason to fight.

First Rule of Childhood Ouchies

The amount of crying increases with the number of people present when the injury occurs.

Corollary:
If nobody's around, it doesn't hurt.

Second Rule of Childhood Ouchies

If you decide not to take your kid to the doctor, it's probably broken.

Third Rule of Childhood Ouchies

Kids can never tell you exactly where it hurts.

Fourth Rule of Childhood Ouchies

Sticks and stones do break bones.

Solomon's Dilemma

Sometimes, you can't be sure who did it.

The Law of the Referee Mom

"He hit me first" is always spoken in stereo.

The Great Cop-Out ⇨

When in doubt, say, "Go ask Dad."

Law of the Third Eye: No matter where they are, parents can see all wrongdoing.

The Pushover Principle

Persistence can turn a mother's no into a yes.

Corollary:
The busier she is, the more likely Mom will say yes.

Corollary:
When all else fails, whine.

The Pushover Alternate Plan

If Mom says no, Dad will say yes.

Corollary:
If both Mom and Dad say no, Grandpa will say yes.

Corollary:
The babysitter will let you get away with anything.

8 / Murphy the Menace

The Flush Tendency

Children stop flushing the toilet when company comes.

The First Clue ⇨

Quiet means trouble.

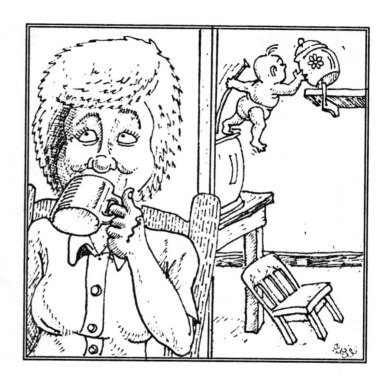

The Home Alone ⇨
Realization

The most innocent-looking child is the one to watch out for.

Law of the Runaway Buick

A child playing in the car parked in your driveway will only pull one lever—the emergency brake.

Fluffy's Learning Experience

If your cat seems to fear your child, there is a good reason.

The Fit Factor ⇨

Children throw temper tantrums in situations guaranteed to maximize your embarrassment.

Corollary:
The presence of a minister, employer, in-law or schoolteacher increases the chance of a temper tantrum.

The Babysitter's Law

You don't want to know what happened while you were gone.

The Comparison ⇨ Shortfall

While your neighbor's child is a piano prodigy, your own child publicly displays creativity by sticking pencils up his nostrils.

The Child Hear/Child Say Dictum

Profanity heard by children on TV and in movies will be repeated in the presence of a minister.

The Law of the Last-Second Reprieve

If you tell a child you will count to five and then spank if the bad behavior does not stop, the child will wait until you reach five.

The Whining Principle

Spoiled children complain the most.

The Perpetual Postponement Conclusion

"I'll do it later" never gets a bed made.

The "Let's Show Mommy" Proverb

A bird in the hand is better than a frog.

The Dark Side Syndrome

A child who looks like you will only inherit your bad qualities.

The Ear-in/Ear-out Theory

Deafness to parents' instructions increases with age.

The Loophole Law ⇨

Every parental command contains a loophole visible only to children.

The Nail-Biting Axiom

You can't force children to quit bad habits.

Corollary:

After you stop trying to break your child of a habit, he will quit on his own.

The Hacker Warning

Never let your ten-year-old roam around in your computer.

Disadvantage:

The only person who truly understands how the computer works is your ten-year-old.

9 / The Exasperated Murphy

First Law of Childhood Illness ⇨

Just as one child recovers from the chicken pox and you think your life will get back to normal, another child will get sick.

Second Law of Childhood Illness

If you take a week of vacation to do things around the house, a child will get sick and need to stay home from school.

Third Law of Childhood Illness

Children's illnesses expand to consume all parental vacation time.

Corollary:
Children don't get sick on weekends.

Fourth Law of Childhood Illness

Children don't get sick until going to bed.

Rules of the Telephone

Children never deliver phone messages.

The more important the message, the less chance the child will relay it.

Whining and fussing increase when you receive a long-distance phone call.

Children always want to play in the room where someone is talking on the phone.

The words "Be quiet!" when spoken by a parent who is talking on the phone mean nothing, except that the parent will repeat those words every thirty seconds.

Phyllis's Laws of Musical Lessons

Children don't want to practice until they quit taking lessons.

Children who want to take lessons don't have a piano.

Having a baby grand in the house squelches talent.

The Fifty-Nine-Minute Principle

No child, when ordered to practice the piano for an hour, goes beyond fifty-nine minutes.

The Spinach Casserole Certainty ⇨

When eating at other people's homes, your hosts will prepare foods which your children don't like.

Corollary:
Your children will point this out during the meal.

Barb's Rule
The longer it takes to prepare a meal, the less your kids will like it.

The Broadway Aspiration

If you put down a nonrefundable deposit for dance lessons, your child will lose interest in taking lessons.

The Money Pit Equation

Day-care costs rise to consume all pay raises, and then some.

Law of Checkbook Decay

The orthodontist's rates will increase just before your child's appointment.

The Vocabulary Conspiracy: Children are experts at creating phrases guaranteed to drive parents nuts, such as...

The "Touch of Rotting Melon" Rule

For Christmas, your children will buy you cheap perfume and jewelry which you can't imagine wearing in public.

The One-Sniff Approval

The closer the outfit is to the top of the dirty clothes basket, the greater the chance it will be retrieved and worn again.

Corollary:
Some clothes never get washed.

First Law of Pets

Children love to take care of pets . . . for about a week.

Second Law of Pets

Mary had a little lamb . . . but her mother fed it.

Corollary:
Its fleece was white as snow . . . because Mom cleaned it.

Third Law of Pets

Children prefer pets which require the most care.

Rodent Corollary:
And smell the worst.

Fourth Law of Pets

The more expensive the tropical fish, the more likely it will die.

⇐ Fifth Law of Pets

The smaller it was when it followed Junior home, the larger it will grow.

Seasonal Certainties

If it's winter, you'll find your child's missing Halloween mask.

If it's spring, you'll find your child's missing glove.

If it's summer, you'll find your child's lost school textbook, which you already paid to replace.

If it's fall, you'll find the missing jersey to your son's Little League uniform, for which you already reimbursed the league.

10 / Murphy on Vacation

The Lakefront Proverb

Spare the rod and spoil the bait.

The Cheese Axiom
If your child smiles at the camera, the camera is out of film.

The Ring Toss Rule

At the carnival, your child will want to play the game with the least chance for success.

Corollary:
The bigger the teddy bear, the less chance of winning it.

Corollary:
Any goldfish won at the carnival won't make it through the night.

The Incredible Hulk ⇨ Rule

The more spectacular the scenery, the greater the chance your kids will prefer reading comic books.

Hilton's Admonition ⇨

Given hotel rooms, children will show aptitude for calling room service, ordering in-room movies, dialing long distance, and activating the "magic fingers" and any other available hotel technology which can appear on your bill.

The McDonald's Lament

A plain hamburger takes fifteen minutes longer to make.

Mark's Law of the Mojave Desert

The car's air conditioner will break during the first 20 miles of your family vacation to Arizona.

The Law of Limited Foliage

Emergency potty stops will occur in areas devoid of bushes.

Laws of Asynchronous Bladders

When several children are in the car, they never have to go to the bathroom at the same time.

Children never have to go to the bathroom before you begin a trip.

Rule of Thumb for Family Vehicles

The minivan you just bought to carry your growing family is too tall for the garage.

Corollary:
Any van that will fit in your garage is too small for your family.

The "Stop It!" Futility ⇨

Dad will never pull the car off the road to discipline children, even if he knows he should.

Corollary:
Children know this.

The Turnpike Problem

The amount of sibling fighting is inversely proportional to the availability of places to pull off the road.

11/Murphy Knows Best

The Law of Zero-Based Parenting

Everything that worked on your first child will fail on your second child.

The Dr. Spock Paradox

The degree to which a child is well adjusted and obedient is inversely proportional to the number of childrearing books the parents read.

The Serial Name Syndrome

Parents address their children with every other sibling's name first.

First Law of Parental Guidance

You can't tell a movie by its rating.

Second Law of Parental Guidance

At the theater, refreshments cost more than the movie.

The Theory of Parental Wisdom

Eighty percent of parental advice is good advice; twenty percent is bad advice.

Corollary:
Children ignore eighty percent of parental advice.

The DINK (Double ⇨ Income, No Kids) Principle

People who don't have kids are more likely to give advice about parenting.

Corollary:
And to write books about parenting.

Law of Deferred Leniency

You will let your youngest children get away with things you would never have allowed the older ones to get away with.

Corollary:
Leniency accelerates.

First Rule of Grandparenting

Children become instant angels when grandparents arrive.

Second Rule of Grandparenting

A grandfather is a person who thinks every baby is absolutely adorable, and is grateful to God that the baby isn't his own.

Third Rule of Grandparenting

The more strict the parents, the more lenient the grandparents.

Fourth Rule of Grandparenting ⇨

Grandparents have more patience with your kids than they had with you.

Corollary A:
And give them more freedom than they gave you.

Corollary B:
And more candy.

Corollary C:
And let them stay up later.

Corollary D:
And let them watch just about anything on TV.

Rules for Gullible Parents

Never believe a child who says:

- ☐ "If you let me get a dog, I promise to take care of it."
- ☐ "I'll return it when I'm done."
- ☐ "I don't have anything to wear."
- ☐ "Yes, I washed behind my ears."
- ☐ "Dad said it was okay."
- ☐ "I'll have your daughter back by 10:00."
- ☐ "Can I borrow the car? I just need to go to the store."

Laws of Allowances ⇨

The older the child, the bigger the allowance.

The bigger the allowance, the less appreciated it is.

No allowance is so reasonable that a child can't negotiate it higher.

The Snitch Truth

If Mom says you can't have any, she probably already snuck a bite.

The Law of Generational Redundancy

You can't prevent your children from repeating your mistakes.

Corollary:
The mistakes of one generation are not only repeated in the next generation, but amplified.

The Brat Repetition

Parents who don't remember the past are condemned to let their kids get away with the same things they got away with as kids.

"Better Late than Never" Law of Parenting

By the time you get the hang of parenting, your children are married.

The Macho Prerogative

Behavior which the mother desires in a son will be discouraged by the father as unmanly.

The Square Footage ⇨ Principle

You can't afford a house big enough for your family until your kids leave home.

The Full House Hypothesis

If you have more children than bedrooms, you will combine children in the way most likely to cause conflict.

Corollary:
Siblings with the least compatible personalities will have to share the same bedroom.

12 / Murphy Becomes a Teen

The Adolescent Continuum Warp Principle

All of the rules change when your child becomes a teenager.

Corollary:
Teenagers make the rules.

The Law of Decibel Overload

The louder the music, the greater the intensity of studying.

The Ulterior Motive Tip-Off

If your son volunteers to help with the housework, there's a reason.

Corollary:
He's probably avoiding something which is much more important and urgent . . . like homework.

The Adolescent Presumption

Upon reaching age thirteen, children become more knowledgeable than their parents.

The Phone Constant ⇨

Don't bother answering. It's for your daughter.

The "Cool" Redefinition

Although your teens use most of the same slang words you used as a teen, all of the meanings are different.

The Elbow Grease Axiom

Teens always want to earn money in the past tense.

The Slumber Party Rule

When you arrive at the home of your daughter's slumber party, she will remember something that she forgot to bring and absolutely *must* have.

The Teen Motto

Whatever a parent likes is uncool.

The "A Woman's Work Is Never Done" Revision

A teenager's work never gets done.

Corollary:
Until Mom does it.

The Foolproof Rejoinder

Jesus had long hair.

The Teenager's Rules of Thumb

If Mom wears it, it's not cool.
If Mom hates it, you may be on to something.

The Uh-Huh Rule

A teenager can answer any question with a one-word response.

Corollary:
That word will probably be mumbled unintelligibly.

The Law of Inconvenient Helpfulness

Children only want to help when their parents don't want help.

Corollary:
Teenagers never want to help.

The Dirty Laundry Rule

Your uncommunicative, private teenager who won't open up around you about his or her personal life will freely reveal all of your shortcomings to friends and their parents.

13 / Murphy 90210

Theory of Prom Jitters

The more time you spend making your daughter's prom dress, the greater the chance she and her boyfriend will break up the night before.

Corollary:
If they don't break up, they should.

The Puppy Love Incentive

The dirt indelibly bonded to your son's elbows since he was five will mysteriously disappear just before his first date.

The Infatuation Factor

Puppy love can turn the most pragmatic, logical teenager into a hopelessly irrational airhead.

The Law of Teen Rebellion

If you are frustrated by your teenage son's rebellious streak, take heart: he'll get over it . . . in seven years.

Corollary:
The sulking, rebellious look you despise in your teenager is the same one in your high-school yearbook picture.

Craig's Caution ⇨

Be suspicious when your teenager offers to watch the house while you're away.

Second Law of Teenage Driving

Make sure you're sitting down when you hear your new insurance rates.

Third Law of Teenage Driving

Driver's Ed class makes teenagers self-appointed experts on driving.

Fourth Law of Teenage Driving

The only fearless drivers are sixteen-year-olds.

The Wheels Motivation

All work and no play makes Jack barely able to afford a car when he turns sixteen.

Corollary:
You'll still have to pay his insurance.

The Divided House Principle

Your eighteen-year-old's vote will cancel out your own vote.

Cindy's Rule of Attire

Teenage girls always try on at least three outfits before leaving the house.

Corollary:
The outfit she really wants is in the dirty clothes hamper.

The Hip Revelation

Your daughter looks better in your clothes than you do.

Corollary:
If you can't find the blouse you want to wear, your daughter is wearing it.

The Law of Radical Decay

Yesterday's hippie is today's old fogy.

The Give-an-Inch Principle

If you extend curfew by an hour, your teen will take two hours.

Forstrom's Late Nite Law

Teenagers never come home before curfew.

Corollary:
No teen can sneak into the house after curfew without waking the parents.

Forstrom's Excuse:
What teens say they were doing after curfew: "Nothing."

The Pseudo-Empty Nest Rule

The closer the college is to home, the greater the chance your child will be accepted there and commute. Unless that's what you want.

The Law of Maytag Reunions: Independent-minded children who move into their own apartment will return frequently... with dirty laundry.